GUNTHER SCHULLER
DUO SONATA

FOR CLARINET
AND BASS CLARINET

ISBN 0-634-01389-0

Associated Music Publishers, Inc.

DISTRIBUTED BY

HAL•LEONARD®
CORPORATION
7777 W. BLUEMOUND RD. P.O. BOX 13819 MILWAUKEE, WI 53213

Duo Sonata

For Clarinet and Bass Clarinet

Gunther Schuller

I

AMP-7407

5 5

II

AMP-7407

6

III

Allegro (♩ = 92-96)

GUNTHER SCHULLER
DUO SONATA

FOR CLARINET
AND BASS CLARINET

ISBN 0-634-01389-0

Associated Music Publishers, Inc.

DISTRIBUTED BY

HAL•LEONARD®
CORPORATION
7777 W. BLUEMOUND RD. P.O. BOX 13819 MILWAUKEE, WI 53213

Duo Sonata

For Clarinet and Bass Clarinet

Gunther Schuller

AMP-7407

II

III

Allegro (♩ = 92-96)

13

AMP-7407